*Government
Knowledge Series*

How to Develop a Winning Small Business Innovation Research (SBIR) Proposal

By Eric Adolphe & Michael Lisagor

Copyright 2015 Government Proposal Solutions, Inc.

All rights reserved

Printed in the United States of America

10 9 8 7 6 5 4 3 2 1

Library of Congress Cataloging-in-Publication Data

Government Contracting Knowledge Series: How to Develop a Winning Small Business Innovation Research (SBIR) Proposal

Eric Adolphe & Michael Lisagor

ISBN-13: 978-1515348085

ISBN-10: 1515348083

Contents

INTRODUCTION 5
STEP 1: SBIR PROCESS OVERVIEW 7
STEP 2: WRITING BASICS 13
STEP 3: IDENTIFICATION & SIGNIFICANCE 21
STEP 4: TECHNICAL OBJECTIVES 31
STEP 5: WORK PLAN 33
STEP 6: RELEVANT EXPERIENCE 39
STEP 7: COMMERCIALIZATION PLAN 41
STEP 8: KEY PERSONNEL & RESUMES 45
STEP 9: COST PROPOSALS 49
STEP 10: PHASE III PROPOSALS 51
SBIR PROPOSAL EVALUATION 55
ABOUT THE AUTHORS 57
ABOUT GOVPROP.COM 59

Introduction

Welcome to *How to Develop a Winning Small Business Innovation Research (SBIR) Proposal*, part of the *Government Proposal Solutions, Inc. Government Contracting Knowledge Series.*

The process companies are required to understand and follow to win federal, state and local government contracts is often confusing and unforgiving. The purpose of this series is to share knowledge, best practices, and lessons learned with the contractor, grantee, consultant and freelance community in conjunction with the services available at www.GOVPROP.com.

SBIR Proposal Development

Step 1: SBIR process overview

The Small Business Innovation Research (SBIR) Program and its sibling, the Small Business Technology Transfer (STTR) program, are federal initiatives that provide over $2 billion in grants and contracts each year to small and start-up companies to develop new or enhanced products and services based on advanced technologies.

About 40% of the SBIR Phase I awards made each year go to firms with no prior SBIR experience. SBIRs are administered by 10 federal agencies for the purpose of helping to provide early-stage Research and Development funding to small technology companies (or individual entrepreneurs who form a company).

Solicitations are released periodically from each of the agencies and involve technical R&D topics that the agency is interested in funding. Companies are invited to compete for funding by submitting proposals answering the technical topic needs of the agency's solicitation. Each of these ten agencies has various needs and variations of the SBIR program. You can learn more about them by visiting their web sites.

SBIR Proposal Development

Eligibility and Application (Proposal) Requirements:

1. To receive SBIR funds, each awardee of a SBIR Phase I or Phase II award must qualify as an SBC (less than 500 employees).
2. For Phase I, a minimum of two-thirds of the research or analytical effort must be performed by the awardee. Occasionally, deviations from this requirement may occur, and must be approved in writing by the funding agreement officer after consultation with the agency SBIR Program Manager/Coordinator.
3. For Phase II, a minimum of one-half of the research or analytical effort must be performed by the awardee. Occasionally, deviations from this requirement may occur, and must be approved in writing by the funding agreement officer after consultation with the agency SBIR Program Manager/Coordinator.
4. For both Phase I and Phase II, the primary employment of the Principal Investigator (PI) must be with the SBC at the time of award and during the conduct of the proposed project.
5. For both Phase I and Phase II, the R/R&D work must be performed in the United States.

SBIR Proposal Development

Proposal Requirements

An SBC submitting a proposal for a funding agreement for Phase I of an SBIR Program that has received more than fifteen Phase II SBIR awards during the preceding five fiscal years must document the extent to which it was able to secure Phase III funding to develop concepts resulting from previous Phase II SBIR awards. Note: SBIR proposal mills are discouraged!

Commercialization Plan. A commercialization plan must be included with each proposal for an SBIR Phase II award moving toward commercialization. Elements of a commercialization plan may include the following:

- Company information: Focused objectives/core competencies; size; specialization area(s); products with significant sales; and history of previous Federal and non-Federal funding, regulatory experience, and subsequent commercialization.
- Customer and Competition: Clear description of key technology objectives, current competition, and advantages compared to competing products or services and description of hurdles to acceptance of the innovation.
- Market: Milestones, target dates, analyses of market size, and estimated market share after first year sales and after five years; explanation of plan to obtain market share.

9

SBIR Proposal Development

- Intellectual Property: Patent status, technology lead, trade secrets or other demonstration of a plan to achieve sufficient protection to realize the commercialization stage and attain at least a temporal competitive advantage.
- Financing: Plans for securing necessary funding in Phase III.
- Assistance and mentoring: Plans for securing needed technical or business assistance through mentoring, partnering, or through arrangements with state assistance programs, SBDCs, Federally-funded research laboratories, Manufacturing Extension Partnership centers, or other assistance providers.
- Data Collection: Each Phase II applicant will be required to provide information to the Tech-Net Database System (htto:// tech-net.sba.gov).

Federal and State Technology (FAST) Partnership Program and Outreach Program

Public Law 106-554, established the Federal and State Technology Partnership Program (FAST Program) to strengthen the technological competitiveness of SBCs in the United States. Congress found that programs that foster economic development among small high-technology firms vary widely among the States.

The purpose of the FAST Program is to improve the participation of small technology firms in the

SBIR Proposal Development

innovation and commercialization of new technology, thereby ensuring that the United States remains on the cutting-edge of research and development in the highly competitive arena of science and technology. SBA administers the FAST Program.

Responsibilities of Small Business Administration (SBA):

SBA's Office of Technology will annually obtain available information on the current critical technologies from the National Critical Technologies panel and the Secretary of Defense and provide such information to the SBIR agencies. SBA will request this information in June of each year. The data received will be submitted to each of the participating Federal agencies and will also be published in the September issue of the SBIR Pre-Solicitation Announcement.

Examples of SBIR Areas to be monitored by SBA:

1. SBIR Funding Allocations. The Act defines the SBIR effort (R/R&D), the source of the funds for financing the SBIR Program (extramural budget), and the percentage of such funds to be reserved for the SBIR Program (3.0 percent). The Act requires that SBA monitor these annual allocations.
2. The accomplishment of scheduled SBIR events, such as SBIR Program solicitation re-

SBIR Proposal Development

leases and the issuance of funding agreements. SBA monitors these and other operational features of the SBIR Program. SBA does not plan to monitor administration of the awards except in instances where SBA assistance is requested and is related to a specific SBIR project or funding agreement.

3. SBA monitors whether follow- on non-Federal funding commitments obtained by Phase II awardees for Phase III were considered in the evaluation of Phase II proposals as required by the Act.

4. SBA monitors whether or not agencies consider Phase III awards for their contracting requirements. The SBA has the ability to challenge the agency's decision.

5. SBA's monitoring activity also includes review of policies, rules, regulations, interpretations, and procedures generated to facilitate intra- and interagency SBIR program implementation.

SBIR Proposal Development

Step 2: Writing basics

There are whole series of writing guidelines that apply specifically to developing a successful SBIR proposal.

Understand the big picture before you begin writing.

- Understand the whole project from start to finish, from feasibility to commercialization. Phase I makes a logical starting point for Phase II, and Phase II creates a basis for Phase III.
- Understand what resources (people, equipment, subcontractors, commercialization partners, money, etc.) are needed along the way, and when they will be identified and secured.
- Understand why the project should be undertaken, what will be the outcome or benefit of the Phase III, both to the market and to your company.
- Understand whether the Phase II effort will allow you to complete all of the necessary R&D (or whether Phase III needs to finish the R&D before progressing to commercialization, and where that Phase III R&D money is going to come from), what the Phase III market is, and down what commercialization path

13

you need to travel to exploit that Phase III opportunity. In other words, get a handle on how to estimate the Phase III market.

Put a lot of thought into your objectives and work plan in your Phase I or Phase II proposal. Reviewers are looking for details.

But don't overlook the big picture.

Here is an example of an SBIR abstract:

Plastic media blast (PMB) is rapidly growing as a coating removal method because it does not damage composite or soft metal surfaces when compared with the effects of chemical stripping solvents or hard abrasives (i.e., sand), however, the conventional PMB materials are all highly resistant to biodegradation. A commercially available, biodegradable plastic known as PHBV and manufactured by ABC Industries is proposed as a biodegradable plastic media blast (BPMB). This new class of biodegradable polymers has several unique features which make it an ideal candidate as a BPMB: (1) microorganisms rapidly biodegrade it to CO_2 and water, (2) it is not affected by water or humidity like starch-blast media, (3) like conventional thermoplastics, it can be melted, molded or extruded, and (4) different hardness characteristics can be engineered into the polymer formulations. It has outlined a comprehensive Phase I *project for conversion of raw PHBV into 20-30 mesh abrasive, testing and evaluation of coating removal characteristics using established procedures for PMB application, documenting biodegradation features, and performing a cost analysis for transitioning this new material to commercial production and application.*

So, identify the problem, provide a solution to the problem, explain why the solution will work, present a plan to demonstrate the solution and, finally, identify the benefits of the solution.

Compliance:

Besides having a true innovation to begin with, compliance is perhaps the single most important predictor of an SBIR win or loss. The level of competition has increased significantly from a 1 in 7 chance of winning, to 1 in 16, to perhaps 1 and 32 today. Here are some tips:

- Read, understand and follow the agency's instructions. Also known as the "funding opportunity announcement (FOA)."
- More than 10% of proposals received by agencies are thrown out because they fail to comply with instructions.
- Use an administrative person who does not care about the innovation to screen the proposal and make sure that it meets minimum standards. Do this before a technical review.

- Agencies change their instructions all of the time. Check instructions before you start the proposal every time.
- Assign a compliance gadfly, someone who is very detail oriented and critical, to review the proposal before it goes out. The gadfly should be looking for any minor inconsistencies between your proposal and the Government instructions. They should not be qualified to comment on the technical merit of the innovation, nor should they be someone who gets starry eyed about new technologies.

Things to Say and Not to Say:

- PI is a Full Time Employee of the SBIR Company - don't contradict this statement.
- Work will be performed in the U.S. - don't contradict this statement.
- The proposal indicates that a prototype will be produced at the end of Phase I. The commercialization discussion describes how the great product will appear on Wal-Mart shelves everywhere. However, the proposal does not show how much money it will take, where the money will come from (see Commercialization section).
- "We will" - instead, state who is doing the work (e.g. PI, Consultant, etc.).
- Proposal shows biography of a consultant, but the cost proposal does not provide a budget for the consultant.

SBIR Proposal Development

Things to Say - Emphasize America:

- SBIRs/STTRs are reserved for American Business.
- All work should be done in the U.S.
- Buy American products and services to do the work.
- Ideally, the work will have a major impact of National Significance - e.g. encourage manufacturers to move back to the U.S., help the war fighter, deny the enemy, etc.

Things to Say – Feasibility:

Weave feasibility into your Phase I proposal. Even though there is not a feasibility section, it is very important and actually is the justification for the Government putting money into risky innovations (they don't know if it will really work). Feasibility is not one issue. It is the main purpose of the project and should be reflected throughout the proposal:

The Abstract: Show the reviewer from the start that you are focused on feasibility by including a statement in the abstract along the lines of "The goal of this Phase 1 project is to prove the feasibility of..."

- Identification and Significance: After stating the problem or opportunity and its importance, explain briefly how your innovative

solution will solve the problem, and how you need to go about proving feasibility.
- Work Plan: If you have indicated the questions that you must answer to prove feasibility, then the work plan can now focus on the specific tasks that you must accomplish to answer those questions. This section also should include a task in which you take all the data and information gathered in the Phase I effort, compare it against your feasibility criteria, and conclude whether feasibility has been proven.
- Related R&D Section: You should talk about the research done by yourself or others that offers insight into why your approach might be feasible, while making sure that you distinguish between what you or others have done versus what you plan to do in this project. Don't leave the impression that you have already proven feasibility.
- Future R&D Section: Summarize how the feasibility effort in Phase I sets the stage for the Phase 2 work that you envision.
- Key Personnel Section: Demonstrate that you have the right people (including subcontractors and consultants) to conduct the Phase I feasibility study.
- Facilities and Equipment Section: Convince the reviewer that you secured the resources necessary to prove feasibility.
- Commercialization Section: Explain that proof of technical feasibility on Phase I repre-

sents a critical milestone in your commercialization process, including your ability to raise capital. Be sure to distinguish the technical feasibility versus the market feasibility.

The DoD has reported a lot of errors in the "Related Research" section of Phase I proposals. Per the instructions, this section is supposed to convince the reviewer that:

- Your team has prior experience relevant to this project.
- You are aware of the state-of-the-art in terms of similar related R&D.

The instructions allow you to submit cost proposals using the format given in the instructions, or the on-line form. Use the on-line form! It enables you to take advantage of "options," and is also more convenient.

Tips On Packaging - Creating Visual Effects:

The quality of delivery of your SBIR proposal will drive the memory retention of the government evaluators. So, pay close attention to the accuracy and quality of proposal graphics.

Step 3: Identification & significance

The successful SBIR proposal will identify and explain the significance of the problem.

Do all the following on the first page:

- Revisit the problem.
- Introduce the basis for the innovation (solution).
- Explain how the solution logically merges with the problem.
- Introduce an overview of the technical objectives -- list specific "global" points.
- Discriminators -- highlight one or two thoughts you really want to impress upon the reviewer.

Provide a background (context) to the problem and solution:

- Explain the problem in detail.
- Explain the innovation in detail.
- Develop premise of why innovation will work.
- Discriminators - How have you positioned yourself using preliminary work or data start out "ahead" in this project?

Here is an example of an SBIR proposal background statement:

SBIR Proposal Development

In the post-September 11th environment, homeland defense and overseas tactical operations require a new generation of surveillance platforms. Current technologies do not satisfy all the requirements of today's security needs. Ground based radar systems are only capable of detecting targets above their horizon line. Targets hiding behind structures or in valleys and ravines cannot be detected. Satellite imagery provides a comprehensive view of targets, however, due to the rotation of the earth, these views only last several minutes. Current UAVs can patrol unlimited locations, but are limited in duration of flight to a matter of hours or days. They are geostationary, reconfigurable, retaskable surveillance platforms that can stay aloft over a target for up to a year or more and be equipped with one optical, radar, and other intelligence surveillance equipment capable of surveying a 700-mile diameter area. And deployed in the theater to detect XXXX weapons and cruise missile attacks, as well as coordination with command. They can be used to perform border patrol tasks such as detecting drug smuggling operations and terrorist incursions.

Here is an example of an identification and significance of the problem section:

With terrorist attacks possible within the United States, such as those that occurred on September

IIth, there is an urgent need for continuous surveillance of the US border. High altitude airships (HAAs) will have the ability to loiter above stationary targets at altitudes over 70,000 feet, well above the jet stream and out of range of enemy defenses (Figure I). For HAAs to remain aloft for up to a year at a time, they must have sufficiently sized energy storage systems requiring no refueling. The most promising energy conversion and storage system for HAAs is the combination of photovoltaic (PV) arrays with a regenerative fuel cell energy storage system. This powers the arrays during the day to power electronics, while utilizing excess power to split water with an electrolyzer, generating hydrogen and oxygen at high pressures. At night, the stored hydrogen and oxygen are fed to a fuel cell where they are converted to electricity, allowing the HAA to continue operation.

The electrolyzer has a significant effect on the specific energy (Wh. kg) of the overall system, affecting the size of the reactant storage based on its operating pressure, and affecting the size of PV arrays needed based on its operating efficiency. The conditions at which the electrolyzer operates, such as temperature and pressure, can also dramatically affect the electrolyzer's balance-of-plant mass and parasitic power requirements. Operating at high pressure reduces the amount of water vapor present in the gas phase, reducing and simplifying water knockout systems. The high pressure also allows for operation at high temperature due to the increased temperature for vaporization of water at elevated pressures. The higher temperature increases the efficiency of electrolysis process reducing the size of PY arrays needed. To take advantage of operating at higher temperature and pressure, development of both membrane electrode assemblies and lightweight electrolyzer stack components are needed that can operate at high temperature and pressure. Although there has been much research on high temperature PEM fuel cells, there has been little focus on high temperature PEM electrolysis, especially at high pressures and with lightweight hardware suitable for flight platforms.

For Phase I, the Center proposes to demonstrate the feasibility of an electrolyzer capable of operating at high pressure (>1000 psig) and high temperature (>100 °C). The Center will contribute to the project by developing the high temperature membrane electrode assembly to be used in an electrolyzer and develop the lightweight electrolyzer component technology that will be capable of functioning at pressures up to 1000 psig and temperatures greater than 100 and contribute by performing a system-level analysis focusing on the effect of high temperature and high pressure on the system efficiency, weight, complexity, and reliability. Phase I will include a demonstration of electrolyzer opera-

tion at 1000 psig and a temperature greater than 100 °C leading to a full-size electrolyzer stack development effort in Phase II.

The identification and significance section of the SBIR is your one and only shot at getting the reviewer excited about your proposal.

According to an official from the NIH, "It doesn't matter how good your approach is, how innovative the idea is, how great the Pl/team is, or how excellent the research facilities are - if what you are proposing lacks significance or has no relevance to the agency mission." This is the "so what?" test. In other words, how does that work make the world a better place? Who benefits? How does it help the war fighter or deny the enemy? How will this make America more productive?

Significance comes in several forms depending on the agency; know the agency that you are writing to. To cover all the points of significance, answer the following questions: What is the innovation? What benefit comes from it? Why should anyone care? Why should the reviewer choose your project over another? Why should taxpayer dollars support this effort?

SBIR Proposal Development

Examples of Significance:

- Social significance – Makes the world a better place, helps people lead happier productive lives, ends hunger or ignorance, etc.
- Research significance - Enables scientific breakthroughs, gives researchers an important tool, or answers a question that other scientists or engineers need to advance other projects.
- National significance - e.g. Encourages manufacturers to move to the U.S., help the war fighter, reduce energy consumption, etc.
- Personal significance - Burning desire to solve a problem that personally impacts the writer.
- Which significance is best? That depends on the agency and the SBIR.

Importance to the Agency:

In addition to the significance, this section also needs to address the importance to the agency receiving your proposal.

General Tips:

- You should not be addressing a "potential problem." Agencies see more real problems that they cannot fund because of budget, so they will probably not fund a potential problem?

SBIR Proposal Development

- Many writers assume that the reader can figure out the significance. Writers spend an inordinate amount of time discussing the technical details and nuances and then take a paragraph of two to explain the significance. Reviewers conclude that if it is not talked about, it must not be significant.
- The innovation has to be significant given the agency's purpose, mission, or priority. It cannot benefit industry and peripherally benefit the Government.
- Don't regurgitate, word for word, the way the topic author wrote up the problem in the solicitation. You must show a deep understanding of the problem and the impact to agency, society, industry, etc.
- Don't introduce 12 things that might be significant with no elaboration on any of them. The reviewer will see lack of focus. There is no magic number (1 - 3) should be a rule of thumb.
- Give plenty of thought to what you will say, and carefully craft the response. This section has to grab the reviewer's attention, get them interested in what your innovation could mean to the agency and the world.

Packaging Tips:

Use of Colors: Colors tend to have an emotional association. Persuasion in the sales process is 50 percent emotion and 50 percent logic. The specific emotional association will vary with the type of audience, individual, and culture.

Blue - Peaceful, soothing, cool authority, power (sometimes) - Backgrounds (90 percent of all business presentations).

Dark shades - often use for printed headings.

White - Neutral, purity, wisdom warm, cheerful - Font color choice for dark background.

Yellow - Warm, cheerful bullets, subheads of dark background
Red - Losses, danger, action, excitement, energy - Bullets and highlights, seldom as a background.
Green - Money, growth, assertive, warmth, comfort - sometimes highlights, occasionally as a background.

Eliminate False Subjects: They displace the true subject of a sentence, waste readers time, and obscure meaning.

Grammar Tips:

- Eliminate Active/Passive Voice. Use active sentences unless you have a good reason to choose passive
- Use a passive sentence when you do not know or do not want to mention the actor

- Use a passive construction to clearly link two sentences
- Use personal pronouns and active voice to convey responsibility and clarity

Step 4: Technical objectives

The most successful SBIR proposals - the ones that often get funded - do a thorough job of helping the government reviewer understand the technical objectives and approach.

Walk the reviewer through the project. A drawing or diagram of the project components is extremely helpful. What is stated on the work plan (tasks) should track with specific objectives and identify tasks or steps needed to demonstrate the innovation and how it applies to the problem solution.

Task descriptions should give the reviewer a guided tour of exactly (step-by-step) what you plan to do for accomplishing each task. Do not leave any room for assumptions by the reviewer. Use recognized procedures or standard methods where possible; this establishes credibility. And, be sure that the work outlined answers the questions but is not impossible to accomplish

Example of Technical Objectives

- Select an available PHBV material with hardness closest to that of conventional PMB Type V (MoH Hardness = 3.5) and process into abrasive grit (mesh size 20 - 30).

SBIR Proposal Development

- Conduct evaluation testing (Air Force Mil. Std. for PMB) using a representative sample (200 lbs.) to obtain parametric data on paint stripping characteristics and effectiveness.
- Prepare a cost analysis based on current market factors (i.e. source material production, processing into PMB, recyclability and disposal cost).
- Preparation and delivery of a final report.
- Option: Actual test demonstration (stripping process) negotiable.

Step 5: Work plan

Often an afterthought, improving the work plan greatly contributes to the success of the proposal.

Here are some hard-earned tips:

- Talk specifics - tell the Government exactly what you are going to do. Answer the following: "who, what, when, where, how and why." This should be done for every task in the Work Plan.
- A common mistake is most proposal writers include WHAT is being done, but don't talk about HOW.
- Read the agency instructions. Some agencies expect up to six pages but the proposer writes one page.
- Make sure that the work plan tasks achieve your objectives.
- It does not sit well with reviewers if the proposal says that you will achieve one thing and the work plan does not include tasks that clearly and logically show how you will achieve it.
- Remember, Phase I is a feasibility study. State what you have to show or prove to demonstrate the feasibility of your innovation idea, and include all of the tasks needed to accomplish the objective.

SBIR Proposal Development

- The agency usually expects you to include a timeline. NSF, for example, mandates that you include a Gantt chart. Some reviewers are skeptical that you can achieve all of the objectives in the work plan. The timeline shows exactly what will be done.
- Include a column on the right that lists the personnel (contractor, consultants, Federal labs, and Universities) that will be involved in each task. For instance, Task 5, Tally results and assess feasibility, will be performed in late month 5 and will be done by John Doe and Jane Smith.

Demonstrate that thought and planning has been directed toward this project:

- Schedule is directly related to tasks.
- Strive for quick startup.
- Show a logical progression of events vs. time. Be reasonable; build in time for Murphy's Law.
- Discriminator: This is the key place where you convince the reviewers that you have a logical, realistic plan that you can successfully execute.

Phase I is a Feasibility Study (or Proof of Concept Analysis). Your idea must be both credible and technically risky (can't be a trivial or evolutionary advancement over the current state of the art).

SBIR Proposal Development

The Phase I proposal needs to define the innovative solution, and what will be done with the $100k, and six months time to convince the agency that your idea has a chance to succeed.

Most writers do not address the feasibility issue that the Phase I proposal will address. Many don't even mention the word "feasibility." Mention feasibility early in the Phase I proposal (see Writing Basics Slides 22 - 24). State what the proposed solution or approach is, and why this is the best possible solution or approach to this problem or opportunity.

Emphasize that you are not certain that your solution or approach will work (the technical risk justifies the Government's use of SBIR funding). Briefly explain why you are uncertain. State how you will decide whether your solution or approach is feasible, and how you will measure feasibility, and finally, justify your feasibility measure.

E.g., if the problem being addressed is treads that keep falling off of Ml tanks, then the proposal should reiterate the unacceptability of this situation for a vehicle engaged in combat You might hypothesize that the material used to make the pins that hold the threads together is failing due to a combination of extreme stress, and abrasion found in sandy environments. Your proposed solution is a new innovative material that can make the pins stronger. Your Phase I project becomes an effort to determine whether this other material is a solution to the tread problem. Prove feasibility in the middle of the project and not towards the end.

The sooner you know about feasibility, the quicker you can complete strategic partnerships. Early determination of infeasibility enables you to redirect the remainder of the Phase I effort.

Your proposal should state that you will test the new material for appropriate strength and abrasion resistance in this application, and that you will deem that the new material is a feasible solution if the material does not fail in at least 99% of the tests you will conduct.

Finally, you should justify using a 99% success rate, and using stress and abrasion conditions that are equal to combat conditions.

Some agencies only accept Phase II proposals from companies that are invited to submit them. The invitation process begins part way through the Phase I effort. Therefore, not concluding feasibility until the end of the Phase I project may hurt your chances for Phase II invitation.

Many DoD agencies have "Fast Track" programs in which Phase I winners can bypass the invitation process and have a very high chance of Phase

II award if they can bring outside funds. The process starts part way through the Phase I project.

Both SOCOM and DHS want to see Phase I projects completed in less than six months. They have problems that they want solved "yesterday."

Some DoD agencies (Army, Navy, and MDO) have Phase I options and can provide additional funding to Phase I winners. However, Phase I options are not exercised until they have selected the firm for Phase II.

While the goal might be to prove feasibility in less than six months, Phase I projects often involve high-risk research and therefore may not go according to plan. Some projects require "no cost extensions" beyond the usual term.

Never sacrifice the quality of a Phase I project just to try to conclude the feasibility in an abbreviated period. If you indicated the questions you must answer to prove feasibility (in the objectives), then the work plan should focus on answering the question(s).

The Work Plan should include a task in which you take all the data and information gathered in the Phase I effort and compare it against your feasibility criteria and conclude whether the feasibility has been proven.

Step 6: Relevant experience

Most SBIR proposal writers misunderstand what is being requested in the Relevant Experience section of the proposal.

They submit boilerplate past performance write-ups with little, if any, edits. However, consider the DoD's instructions:

"Related Work section should include "significant activities directly related to the proposed effort, including any conducted by the Principal Investigator, the proposing firm, consultants, or others. The proposal must persuade the reviewers of the proposer's awareness of the state-of-the-art in the specific topic."

Here are some useful relevant experience writing tips:

This section should describe briefly the experience of the proposing team that is relevant to the proposed topic.

The team includes all employees, consultants and subcontractors. Make sure that there is a balance between the prime and its subcontractors, university partners, or consultants. The ideal is to show that the majority of experience is with the small business.

Highlight the work performed by the Principal Investigator (PI), because you want to take this opportunity to sell the reviewer on the appropriateness and qualifications of the PI. Identify specifically what the PI has done. The Government wants to know why the PI is right for the project.

Demonstrate to the reviewer that you know the state-of-the-art or the significant contributions that others have made in this area. The Government does not want to fund a company that is unaware of what others have done, because s/he wants you to learn from others experience and build on it (and also to avoid any pitfalls others have discovered).

Resist the temptation to over-describe the state of the art. Avoid long-winded descriptions. The reader wants to read enough to know that the company is up to speed. They likely already know the state-of-the-art.

On the other hand, don't be too narrow in your description of the state-of-the-art. You need to cover what others have done in the area of your proposed innovation and also cover what others have done to try to solve the problem you are working on.

Step 7: Commercialization plan

The commercialization plan in the Phase I proposal has gotten increased attention with the SBIR Reauthorization Act. Congress has specifically challenged the DoD to more quickly bring SBIR innovations to the war fighter. Some agencies like NSF also want you to include a 3 to 5 page discussion. NSF also wants at least one (preferably three) letters of support for the technology. Letters (not from techies) should "demonstrate that the company has initiated dialogue with relevant stakeholders (potential customers, strategic partners or investors) for the proposed innovation and that a real business opportunity may exist should the technology prove feasible."

Some agencies are now using commercialization experts on Phase I proposal review teams. So, commercialization must be addressed in Phase I and not as an afterthought:

- Who/What will benefit from the success of this work?
- Develop either a general or specific pathway to commercial use.
- Provide cost analysis data.
- Have solid data for the conventional technology.

- Provide an estimate of the cost of the new process.
- Introduce future plans.
- Give an outline of where you go after this project.
- Develop a plan of how you will interface with an industry partner.

An important commercialization issue is that agencies have different definitions of commercialization:

- Most agencies expect the user to be the agency or a related entity.
- DoD view is that it means making it available for internal use, with special emphasis on getting innovations to the war fighter. Private sector use is of secondary importance.
- NSF's view is that commercialization is private sector only.
- NASA's view is that it should be both internal use and outside of NASA (including other Government agencies).

Read the solicitation very carefully and write the commercialization plan accordingly.

Consider the size of the Phase III opportunity before you decide to pursue a Phase I. Also, consider the company's core competencies and determine if the SBIR can be used effectively to obtain contracts without further competition.

SBIR Proposal Development

Just because a topic is in the SBIR solicitation does not guarantee there is a profitable market, or even that the agency will use the technology internally. You may have to find other markets outside of the agency to make commercialization of your SBIR financially viable.

A few final tips:

- Show that you know the competition.
- Show that you know the market
- Targeting market "influencers" in the commercialization plan.
- Do not look like an SBIR factory.
- Do not pick topics that have little commercialization potential.
- When disclosing previous SBIRs, note that the Government is leery about companies that win Phase I and Phase II proposals and then stop.
- Show what you have done (especially if you have invested your own funds) towards commercialization of prior SBIRs.

Step 8: Key personnel & resumes (including subcontractors & consultants)

Another overlooked area that is vital to the success of the SBIR proposal is key personnel and resumes. Every agency SBIR proposal needs to designate a person who will serve as the principal investigator (PI). Some writers don't name the PI until the very end of the proposal (resumes). By then it is too late. The Government will take a risk on the innovation, but will NOT take a chance on the qualifications of the PI. Put another way, the Government can live with proposed innovation not being feasible, but it cannot be due to the team's incompetence.

Each agency has a different definition for the PI. NASA summarizes the role of the PI as planning and directing the SBIR project; leading it technically and making substantial personal contributions during its implementation; serving as the primary contract with NASA on the project; and ensuring that the work proceeds according to contract agreements. The PI's resume should reflect credibility in each of these roles.

The PI must be primarily employed by the small business that is submitting the proposal. Some agencies provide additional guidance such as:

- NASA: PI must spend at least half of their total employed time with the small company.
- Department of Energy: PI must devote at least a 130 hours to the Phase I project (and a minimum of five hours per week).

Agency requirements are constantly changing. Check with the solicitation.

The Government must trust the qualifications of the PI (ability to innovate, to manage, and to conduct research).

Update resumes for each SBIR. In other words, tailor them to fit the specific SBIR. Generic resumes get generic scores! Make previous work, experience and education relevant to the work plan, objectives, and the innovation and:

- Do not list every paper written, just the relevant ones.
- Show experience in conducting research and in commercialization.
- Confirm that the PI works for the company.
- Keep the resume simple (approximately two pages).
- Explain any gaps in employment.
- Include any business experience.

SBIR resumes typically have focused 99.9% on technology development projects. It should be

60% research, 20% technology development, and 20% business commercialization.

Use consistent resume formats for the entire team. Each resume should be carefully tailored to the project being proposed, and the collective set of resumes (along with qualifications of any subcontractors or consultants) shows to the reviewers that you have all the major bases covered. Consistent formats suggest that everyone on the team is on the same page. Also keeping resumes short and focused helps the reviewer see the relevant qualifications without having to wade through pages of irrelevant text.

Project personnel are a key component of a winning proposal:

- Convince the reviewer that you are the best qualified to carry out the project.
- Involve one or more expert consultants in your project.
- Identify and obtain support from an industrial partner.
- As the Principal Investigator, you are ultimately responsible for the project. So, how and why you are qualified must be described.

Step 9: Cost Proposals

There are several items to consider in an SBIR cost proposal. These include:

- One month of PI time on Phase I. Two months in Phase II.
- Adequate engineering and other technical personnel labor hours.
- Travel must be directly related to carrying out the project.
- Must establish engineering overhead rate and General & Administrative (G&A) rate.
- All direct cost items must be justified.
- Must show ability to capture direct (time sheets) and indirect costs as they occur (purchase orders).
- An accounting system appropriate for government contracts must be in place before a Phase II award can be made.
- Pre-award audits and post-award audits are likely to be made.

SBIR Proposal Development

Step 10: Phase III proposals

SBIR Phase III awards only need to have a relationship with prior SBIR funded agreements that the agency is willing to agree exists.

Under Federal Procurement Regulations (see FAR 6.302-5), it is sufficient to state for purposes of a justification and approval that the project is a SBIR Phase III award and that the product or service is derived from, extends, or logically concludes efforts performed under prior SBIR funding agreements and is authorized under 10 U.S.C. 2304(b)(2) or 41 U.S.C. 253(b)(2). No sole source justification is required.

In fact, the Act requires reporting to SBA of all instances in which an agency pursues research, development, or production of a technology developed by an SBIR awardee, with a concern other than the one that developed the SBIR technology. (See Section 4(c)(7) immediately for agency notification to SBA prior to award of such a funding agreement and Section 9(a)(12) regarding agency reporting of the issuance of such award.) SBA will report such instances, including those discovered independently by SBA, to Congress.

What is interesting about the Phase III language is that it also applies to large prime contractors.

SBIR Proposal Development

So let's say that Lockheed Martin wins a $50 Million contract with the FBI to develop analytics tools. You can go to the prime (Lockheed) and request that they award to you a sole source contract to perform part of that work. Below is the citation:

For Phase III, Congress intends that agencies or their Government-owned, contractor-operated facilities, Federally-funded Research and Development Centers (FRDC), or Government prime contractors that pursue R/R&D or production developed under the SBIR Program, give preference, including sole source awards, to the awardee that developed the technology.

This requirement also applies to technologies of SBIR awardees with SBIR funding from two or more agencies where one of the agencies determines to pursue the technology with an entity other than that awardee.

Notification must include, at a minimum:

- The reasons why the follow-on funding agreement with the SBIR awardee is not practical.
- The identity of the entity with which the agency intends to make an award to perform research, development, or production.

SBIR Proposal Development

- A description of the type of funding award under which the research, development, or production will be obtained.

The SBA may appeal the decision to the head of the contracting activity. If SBA decides to appeal the decision, it must file a notice of intent to appeal with the contracting officer no later than 5 business days after receiving the agency's notice of intent to make award.

Upon receipt of SBA's notice of intent to appeal, the contracting officer must suspend further action on the acquisition until the head of the contracting activity issues a written decision on the appeal.

The contracting officer may proceed with award if he or she determines in writing that the award must be made to protect the public interest.

The contracting officer must include a statement of the facts justifying that determination and provide a copy of its determination to SBA.

Within 30 days of receiving SBA's appeal, the head of the contracting activity must render a written decision setting forth the basis of his or her determination.

SBIR Proposal Development

SBIR proposal evaluation

Government evaluators first review for compliance. Around 10-15 percent of SBIR proposals are eliminated and not even read due to non-compliance with instructions. For instance, 12-point font means 12-point font. Many agencies have implemented software to automate this review.

Next is a peer review, comprised of volunteers from industry, academia, etc. They review SBIR proposals and rank them (score 1-5). They are looking for the following (about 50 percent will make it through this review):

a. Significance of the problem – does the SBIR address a major problem?
b. Qualifications of the Principle Investigator - can he/she pull it off?
c. Innovation - is there real innovation here or just repackaging of existing technologies or products?
d. Approach/Work Plan - does the approach make sense? Are dates and milestones realistic?
e. Facilities - are the necessary facilities and equipment available? If not, can they be accessed through a "Funds in Agreement" (FIA) or by partnering with a University.

SBIR Proposal Development

If the SBIR proposal survives these screens, then the package is sent to a second internal government review team. Typically about 20 percent make it to this point.

Finally, the SBIR proposals that make it through these steps are sent to various potential program offices/sponsors. So, if 50 SBIR proposals were originally received, approximately 5 will be distributed to various program offices to see if any of the Government scientists want to oversee the SBIR.

For the last few years, one agency, the NIH, reported that they did not spend all of their SBIR funds because so few of the submitted proposals made it through the entire process. Which means, "Do your homework and submit a compliant and compelling proposal."

For further information and support, email: support@GOVPROP.com.

SBIR Proposal Development

About the authors

ERIC A. ADOLPHE is the CEO and visionary behind Government Proposal Solutions, Inc. (GPSI – www.GOVPROP™.com). He is a 17 time SBIR Principle Investigator and has written and won SBIRs for NASA, NIH, and DOD. He is also the sole African American SBIR Tibbetts Award Winner and has been a speaker at DOD, SBA, NSF, and NIH SBIR National Seminars and Workshops.

Eric has supported the acquisition of several Government contracting firms and assisted many clients in building best in class bid and proposal and sales organizations that significantly impacted revenue growth. Previously, Eric was founder and CEO of OPTIMUS Corporation and winner of the National Capital Business Ethics Award. He has a JD from the Catholic University of America, Columbus School of Law; and a Bachelor of Engineer in Electrical Engineering from the City College of New York.

MICHAEL LISAGOR is a co-founder and Chief Knowledge Officer at GPSI. Mike is responsible for the development of GOVPROP's online Knowledge Academy. He founded Celerity Works in 1999 to help government contractor executives accelerate their revenue growth. Prior to this, Mike was a domestic and international business development executive for over ten years.

Mike has implemented the bid and proposal process and training program for over 40 government contractors and has reviewed hundreds of competitive proposals. He has completed 75+ organizational assessments and 250+ executive and manager coaching assignments. He established the acquisition risk management process for the GSA FEDSIM organization. Mike has an MS in Management from National Louis University where he taught marketing for managers and a BA in Urban Studies from California State University Northridge. He is also the author of *Managing and Winning Government Business* and *The Enlightened Manager*.

About GOVPROP.com

GOVPROP™.com is a one-stop secure online marketplace connecting federal, state, local and international government contractors and grantees with verified experts and consultants. GOVPROP's aim is to serve and protect both the freelance consultants and the companies hiring them. The design of the system goes right at the pain points on both sides of the equation.

GOVPROP also provides real-time market intelligence, a Knowledge Academy, secure collaboration, expert talent matching and a broad range of related business services. Our expert database includes former government officials and private sector employees who spent years supporting public sector programs. Contractors can search for proposal managers, graphic artists, price to win specialists, contracts specialists, bid protest attorneys, marketing and communications specialists, government affairs specialists, cyber security experts, IT and programming, construction experts, and other skills.

Government Proposal Solutions, Inc.
Info@govprop.com   (888) 385-9346 x102

Made in the USA
Middletown, DE
24 October 2016